The Secret Kingdom

Nek Chand, a Changing India, and a Hidden World of Art

Barb Rosenstock   *illustrated by* **Claire A. Nivola**

CANDLEWICK PRESS

On the continent of Asia, near the mighty Himalayas, in the
Punjab region of long ago, sat the tiny village of Berian Kalan,
the place Nek Chand Saini called home.

In the village, Nek played and planted, laughed and listened, as the ancient stories circled with the seasons, beginning to end and back again.

In blistering summer fields, his father told of wise kings while they raised scarecrows dressed in torn kurtas and dented bucket hats.

On frosty winter nights, his mother told of graceful goddesses while snuggling him in thick rajai made from scraps of fabric.

During the monsoon rains, his sisters told of magical geese while collecting sticks for toy rafts. And at harvest, his brothers told of fierce jackals and chattering monkeys while picking up each fallen kernel of kanak, wasting nothing.

During the festivals of Diwali and Lohri, traveling minstrels told of hidden temples and secret jungles.

Season by season, Nek's head filled with stories, until it overflowed.

Then on the banks of the village stream, Nek built a world of his own. He dug silt palaces and spilled waterfalls, molded clay goddesses and planted stick kings. He found rocks shaped like jackals, monkeys, and geese, and made them pounce, scamper, or fly.

At midday, his mouth watering
for toasted chapatis, Nek
walked past plowmen singing
behind oxen and bangled
women swaying to balance
water jugs — all following the
curving paths home.

He traveled from stream to home, home to school, and back again. Year after year he watched babies arrive and old ones pass on. Nek became a farmer, part of the ancient cycle of changing seasons and shared stories.

Until the men with guns came.

The Punjab split into two countries: Pakistan and India. People of all faiths had lived together for ages, but now Nek's village was in the Muslim country of Pakistan and his Hindu family no longer belonged.

The Saini family fled at night, walking for twenty-four days across the new border into India. Nek carried only village stories in his broken heart.

In the crowded towns, no one needed another poor farmer, so Nek shoveled gravel to build roads. He found work as a government road inspector and moved to India's first modern city, Chandigarh.

Twenty-six villages were bulldozed flat to build Chandigarh, a sharp-edged city of colorless concrete. Nothing in this modern place tugged at Nek's village heart. *Where were the curving paths and flowing streams? Where were the singing men, the swaying women? Where were the stories?*

Nek dreamed of a place to belong.

At the city's northern edge, he found acres of jungle scrubland owned by the government. Though no building was permitted, Nek began settling this hidden wilderness.

Battling clouds of mosquitoes and slithering cobras, he cut a half acre of dense vegetation and built a mud hut. He set up a wall of official-looking oil drums to say "Keep Out!"

Before work, Nek roamed the roadsides, picking up the broken pieces of village life under the modern city. He gathered chipped sinks, cracked water pots, and broken glass bangles in red, blue, and green. On his bicycle, he collected boulders from faraway riverbeds, some shaped like the people and animals he missed most. After work, he carried these treasures into the wilderness.

Until, seven years later, the time came to build the secret kingdom.

Filling hundreds of used burlap bags with concrete, Nek stacked boulder terraces, mixed cement in dented metal bowls, and colored it with brick dust. He troweled on the wet paste and pressed in porcelain shards chipped from old sinks and toilets, wasting nothing.

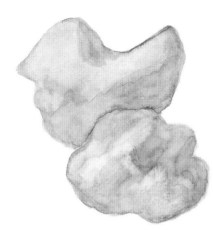

He paved curving paths, carved
niched walls, and strung pebble-
covered wire to make transparent
screens. Fractured tiles or
electric sockets formed archways
bowing to one courtyard, then
another—all connected like the
village he remembered.

Nek saved half-dead plants from the city dump. He filled rusty barrels with water, rolled them in secret to his land, and brought the plants back to life. The secret kingdom filled with flaming bougainvillea, blushing oleander, sweet mango, and tangled pipal trees.

He made skeletons from twisted bikes and rusty pipes, covering their frames in concrete etched with the faces of goddesses and queens. Rows of bangles made rainbows of singing men, swaying women, and laughing children. He sculpted packs of jackals, troops of monkeys, and flocks of geese. Beginning to end and back again, Nek found each group a place to belong, until he belonged too—king of a hidden land of stories.

Nek built his kingdom over twelve acres and kept it secret for fifteen years.

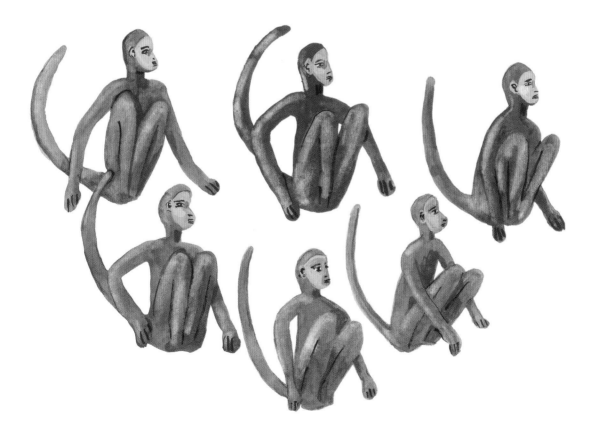

One day, a government crew
clearing jungle underbrush
stumbled onto Nek's land.
They reported his illegal
building to the police.

Everyone in Chandigarh learned
his secret. Officials were outraged.
Nek Chand Saini should lose
his job!

His kingdom would be destroyed.

Until the people of Chandigarh came.

Curious, they entered this magical world created by a humble
road inspector. By the hundreds, city people roamed sculptured
walkways, ducked through arches, laughed and told village stories,
beginning to end and back again.

insisted on its protection. Dr. M. S. Randhawa, a biologist and anthropologist who was chief commissioner and chairman of the Landscape Committee in Chandigarh, recognized the value of Chand's artwork, supported the collection, and advocated for its protection. In 1976, the city promoted Nek Chand to director of the official "Rock Garden" in Chandigarh, which then opened to the public.

He continued to build an extensively landscaped second phase of his kingdom—constructing waterfalls, bridges, and streams—which was completed in 1983. Chand also started a program for citizens and industries in Chandigarh to recycle household and industrial waste to be used in his art.

Though Nek Chand was awarded India's Padma Shri, naming him a national treasure, in 1984, some officials still objected to his recycled artwork and threatened its destruction. In 1990, hundreds of demonstrators, including many children, formed a human chain to stop bulldozers from destroying the site. In 1996, while Nek Chand visited the United States to speak at art museums and galleries, officials stopped funding and the site was vandalized. City agreements to protect the site are not always honored. As a result, the Rock Garden is deteriorating.

The Nek Chand Foundation was formed in 1997 by a group of artists, conservators, and the public to support Nek Chand's work and awareness of the Rock Garden. Chand's artwork has been exhibited in Europe, the United States, and Asia. It can be found in the Collection de l'art Brut in Switzerland, the Collectie De Stadshof in Belgium, and in the U.S. at the American Folk Art Museum, the American Visionary Art Museum, the Museum of International Folk Art, and the John Michael Kohler Arts Center, which owns the largest collection outside Chandigarh.

Until his death in 2015 at age ninety, Nek Chand spent each day at home in the Rock Garden meeting with visitors, creating new plans, and supervising the continued construction of his kingdom.

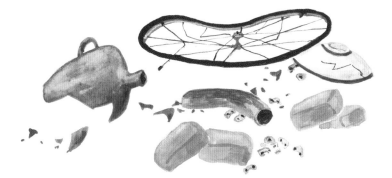

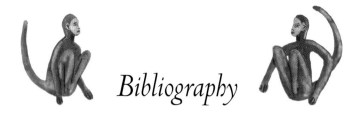

Bibliography

Anderson, Brooke Davis. "Nek Chand Exhibition and Talk." Indo-American Arts Council, June 15, 2006. http://www.iaac.us/nek_chand/nek_chand.htm.

———. "Concrete Kingdom: Sculptures by Nek Chand." *Folk Art*, Spring/ Summer 2006, 42–49.

Bagla, Pallava. "India's Vast Trash Garden a Monument to Recycling." *National Geographic News*, October 7, 2002.

Bandyopadhyay, Soumyen, and Iain Jackson. *The Collection, the Ruin and the Theatre: Architecture, Sculpture and Landscape in Nek Chand's Rock Garden, Chandigarh.* Liverpool: Liverpool University Press, 2007.

Chandigarh Industrial and Tourism Department. "Rock Garden." http://www .citcochandigarh.com/places_to_visit.html.

Cox, Paul, and Ulli Beier. *The Kingdom of Nek Chand.* New York: Raw Vision, 1985. VHS.

Crossette, Barbara. "Le Corbusier's Chandigarh." *New York Times*, April 25, 1982, 523.

Irish, Sharon. "Intimacy and Monumentality in Chandigarh, North India: Le Corbusier's Capitol Complex and Nek Chand Saini's Rock Garden." *Journal of Aesthetic Education* 38, no. 2 (Summer, 2004), 105–115.

Jackson, Iain. "Nek Chand's Rock Garden, Chandigarh India." http://myweb .tiscali.co.uk/iainjackson/nekchand_info/index.html.

Johnson, Ken. "Concrete Cosmos of Bits and Pieces." *New York Times*, August 11, 2006. http://www.folkartmuseum.org/content/uploads/2014/08 /Chand_NYT.pdf.

Kahn, Yasmin. *The Great Partition: The Making of India and Pakistan.* New Haven: Yale University Press, 2008.

Kaufman, Michael T. "Correspondent's Choice: Nek Chand's Garden Fantasy." *New York Times*, April 3, 1983, 16.

Magnier, Mark. "In India, a Secret Garden that Rocks." *Los Angeles Times*, December 6, 2011.

Mahoney, Robert. "Hoard of Trash Becomes Works of Art: Indian Elevates Garbage to Sculpture." *Los Angeles Times,* January 31, 1988.

Maizels, John. "25 Years of Nek Chand's Rock Garden." *Raw Vision,* 35 no. 23 (1997).

———. "Nek Chand, Creator of a Magical World." In *Vernacular Visionaries: International Outsider Art.* Edited by Annie Carlano. New Haven: Yale University Press, 2006.

———. *Raw Creation: Outsider Art and Beyond.* London: Phaidon, 1996.

Maizels, John, S. S. Bhatti, and P. Reeve. *Nek Chand Shows the Way.* New York: Raw Vision, 1997. Exhibition Catalog.

Mehta, V. P. and Nek Chand Saini. *Rock Garden: A Vision of Creativity.* Chandigarh: Arun, 2011.

Nek Chand Foundation website. www.nekchand.com.

Oppenhimer, Ann. "Nek Chand's Rock Garden." *Folk Art Messenger* 19 no. 3 (Fall/Winter 2007). http://www.folkart.org/mag/nek-chand-2.

Peiry, Lucienne, Philippe Lespinasse, and John Maizels. *Nek Chand's Outsider Art.* Paris: Flammarion, 2006.

Rajer, Tony. Interview by Jason Church, *Preservation Technology Podcast,* https://ncptt.nps.gov/blog/podcast-tony-rajer-on-folk-art-conservation-and-the-rock-garden-in-chandigarh-india/.

Russell, Charles. *Groundwaters: A Century of Art by Self-Taught and Outsider Artists.* New York: Prestel, 2011.

Schiff, Bennett. "A Fantasy Garden by Nek Chand Flourishes in India." *Smithsonian* 15 no. 3 (June, 1984), 126.

Umberger, Leslie. *Nek Chand: Healing Properties.* John Michael Kohler Arts Center, 2000. Exhibition Catalog.

———. *Sublime Spaces and Visionary Worlds: Built Environments of Vernacular Artists.* New York: Princeton Architectural Press, 2007.

To M. C. R., D. E. R., and J. J. R.—
there's no place like home.
B. R.

For Pietro, my only brother and dearer to me
than anyone other than he can understand.

And for Peter Chermayeff, our friend,
who first told me about Nek Chand.
C. N.

Acknowledgments

Sincere thanks to John Maizels, Alan Cesarano, Christine Style, John Cross of the Nek Chand Foundation, and Soyna Gulhati for their careful reading of the manuscript and valuable suggestions. Much appreciation to Karen Patterson, associate curator, and the staff at the John Michael Kohler Arts Center for introducing me to outsider art and the sculptures of Nek Chand.

The utmost honor and respect to Nek Chand for his artistic vision, his creative spirit, and his hard work in building and sustaining the Rock Garden of Chandigarh, a gift to the world.

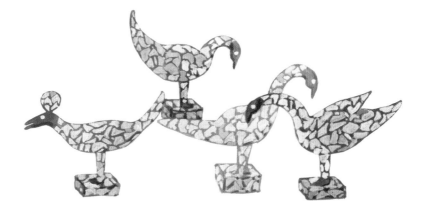

To help preserve and protect Nek Chand's Rock Garden
in Chandigarh, please contact:

The Nek Chand Foundation
P.O. Box 44
Watford, WD25 8LN, United Kingdom
www.nekchand.com

Text copyright © 2018 by Barb Rosenstock
Illustrations copyright © 2018 by Claire A. Nivola

First edition 2018

Library of Congress Catalog Card Number pending
ISBN 978-0-7636-7475-5

17 18 19 20 21 22 APS 10 9 8 7 6 5 4 3 2 1

Printed in Humen, Dongguan, China

This book was typeset in Centaur.
The illustrations were done in watercolor and gouache.

Candlewick Press
99 Dover Street
Somerville, Massachusetts 02144

visit us at www.candlewick.com